HERMAN'S
hiding places

Written by Karen Emigh
Illustrated by Steve Dana

Herman's Hiding Places
All marketing and publishing rights guaranteed to and reserved by

FUTURE HORIZONS INC.

800-489-0727
817-277-0727
817-277-2270 (fax)
www.FHautism.com

ISBN 13: 978-1-935274-61-2

For Bryce,
who is all snakes, snails and
puppy dog tails and a complete joy.
No one could ask for a better brother or son.
I love you, Goose!

Can you find Herman on each page?

Hi! I'm Brett.

My dog Herman and I are going to play
hide and seek. There is just one problem.
Herman doesn't like to stay in one place too long.
He likes to trick me by moving from one place
to another. If you help,
maybe we can find
him together.

Let's count to 10 so Herman can hide.
Ready? 1...2...3...4...5...6...7...8...9...10.
Okay. Let's find Herman.

Maybe he is  the hill? No.

What about  the doghouse?

How about  the toy box?

Let's look  the tub.

What about **UNDER** the steps?

He could be

the curtains.

Let's take a look

BEHIND

the fence.

He has to be **BEHIND** the chair.

We haven't had very good luck
finding Herman.
Let's look in Bryce's room.

We did it! We found Herman.
I guess he got sleepy, because there he is
UP the ladder, **IN** bed, **UNDER** the covers,
and **BEHIND** Bryce, taking a nap.

Thanks for helping me find Herman.
I hope you will join us
on another adventure soon!

A NOTE TO PARENTS

Repetitive cues (whether they are physical, verbal, and/or visual) help concepts fix themselves in a child's rote memory. Here are some examples you can practice with your child in your everyday routine.

When making the bed, put a blanket over your head and tell your child, "I'm under the blanket!" Then, pull it off and say, "I'm out of the blanket." Or, hide behind the couch and say, "I'm behind the couch." Come out and sit on the couch and say, "Now, I'm on the couch."

There are opportunities everywhere, such as in the grocery store and in your kitchen.

You can do this with many prepositions such as out, over, on, around, etc. Use your imagination and be silly. Kids love that! Try it and you'll find this can be a fun game for everyone. Your child will not know you're teaching important concepts to him or her.

Good luck and best wishes.

— Karen

ABOUT THE AUTHOR & ILLUSTRATOR

Karen Emigh and her husband Ken are the parents of two boys, Brett and Bryce. Karen began writing children's books as a way to help Brett, who was diagnosed with an autism spectrum disorder, to better understand abstract language.

Steve Dana and his wife Jodie are the parents of Eric and Kelsey. Karen and Steve have been friends since primary school and reside in the same town in Northern California.

Who took my shoe?

Don't miss the first in the series
written by Karen Emigh and Illustrated by Steve Dana

This wonderfully written book and its colorful illustrations will help your child discover the concepts of "who," "what," "where," "when," "why," and "how." These abstract concepts are often difficult for special needs children to understand.

A great learning tool! Kids won't even realize that they're learning difficult concepts because reading it (or listening to it being read to them) is so much fun!

Play hide and seek with Herman in your own house!

Carefully cut out Herman and hide him, and then see if other people can find him. Remember to use the words **Up, Under, Behind,** and **In** when you give clues about where Herman is hiding!

Printed in the USA
CPSIA information can be obtained
at www.ICGtesting.com
JSHW060049150824
68134JS00031B/2698